The Story of…

PIZARRO
AND THE INCAS

Author
NICK SAUNDERS

ticktock

THE CAST

Francisco Pizarro: *1475-1541. Born an illegitimate son of Gonzalo Pizarro (senior), Francisco was the eldest brother of Gonzalo Pizarro (junior), Juan Pizarro and Hernando Pizarro. He was also the second cousin of Hernando Cortés, who conquered the Aztec Empire. Pizarro sailed to the New World in 1502, landing in the West Indies and lived on the island of Hispaniola. His first expedition in 1524 was unsuccessful, but his second (1526) and third (1529) voyages brought rich rewards. Between 1532-1534 he conquered the Inca Empire in Peru.*

Diego de Almagro: *1475-1538. Conquistador comrade of Francisco Pizarro who lost an eye in fighting Amerindians in Colombia. He accompanied Pizarro on the conquest of the Inca Empire, fell out with him, then led the European discovery of Chile. He returned to Peru, seized Cuzco for himself, and was then defeated in battle by Hernando Pizarro.*

Atahualpa: *1502-1533. Illegitimate son of the Inca emperor Huayna Capac, whose power base was at Quito in Ecuador. Pizarro captured him at Cajamarca in 1532, ransomed him for treasure, and then executed him. Atahualpa was the thirteenth and last emperor of the Inca Empire.*

Hernando Pizarro: *1501-1578. Legitimate half-brother of Francisco Pizarro, Hernando was well educated, arrogant, and well connected in royal circles. He ruled Cuzco with his brothers Juan and Gonzalo, and executed Almagro in 1538. Convicted of murder, he was imprisoned for 20 years in Spain.*

Gonzalo Pizarro: *1506-1548. Gonzalo was the younger half-brother of Francisco Pizarro. Tough and cruel, Gonzalo mistreated the Incas, and caused Manco Inca's rebellion in 1536. He helped defeat Almagro in 1537, and led a disastrous expedition to search for golden El Dorado in 1540. He later rebelled against Spanish rule, and was defeated and executed in 1548.*

Copyright © ticktock Entertainment Ltd. 2006
First published in Great Britain in 2006 by ticktock Media Ltd.,
Unit 2, Orchard Business Centre, North Farm Road, Tunbridge Wells, Kent, TN2 3XF
ISBN 1 84696 041 X
Printed in China
We would like to thank David Drew.
A CIP catalogue record for this book is available from the British Library.

CONTENTS

THE SPANISH EMPIRE

In the 16th century, Spain was the most powerful country in Europe, and a bitter Catholic enemy of Protestant England. Spain carved out a vast colonial empire in the Americas beginning with Hernan Cortés who conquered the Aztec Empire, in Mexico, in 1521. South America was almost unknown at the time, but persistent rumours of a great golden kingdom south of Panama drew Francisco Pizarro and others to explore the uncharted region. What they discovered surpassed even Mexico's riches.

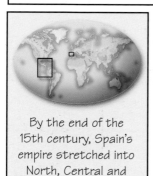

By the end of the 15th century, Spain's empire stretched into North, Central and South America.

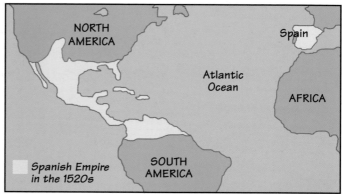

Spanish Empire in the 1520s

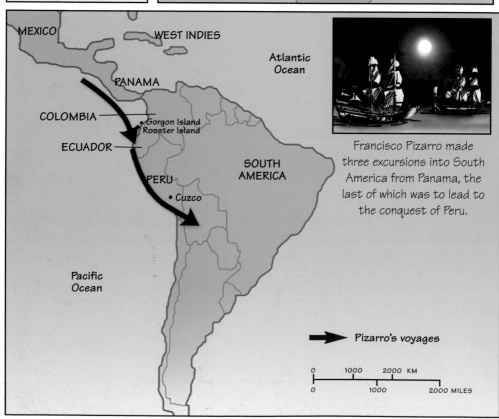

Francisco Pizarro made three excursions into South America from Panama, the last of which was to lead to the conquest of Peru.

Pizarro's voyages

Spanish conquistadors were among the toughest, best armed and most ruthless soldiers in Europe at the time. Their armour, swords, arquebus, cannon and expert horsemanship made them the terror of their European enemies.

Spanish forces led by Pizarro would eventually come face to face with the Inca Empire. It was the largest and most successful of all native American civilisations. Despite this, their tools and weapons were mainly stone and bronze, and firearms and even horses were unknown. The Incas also had no immunity to the terrible diseases that Europeans brought with them, such as smallpox.

A HUMBLE BIRTH

Francisco Pizarro's illegitimate birth and poor education made him a natural choice to become a conquistador, who would leave Spain to seek fortune and fame in the Americas. His humble beginnings made his eventual rise to become one of most successful and notorious conquerors of the Americas all the more surprising.

Francisco Pizarro was born sometime in 1475, in the city of Trujillo, in the Extremadura region of Spain. He was the illegitimate son of Gonzalo Pizarro, a soldier, and Francisca. Francisco was the eldest of three brothers, the others were Gonzalo, Juan and Hernando, all of whom were to accompany him in his conquest of the Inca Empire.

Francisco's father, Gonzalo, was a distinguished soldier, who fought as a colonel of infantry in Spain and Italy. He left his family alone for long periods of fighting.

Take care, Gonzalo! Hurry back to us.

Goodbye, father. I will miss you!

Francisco was the second cousin of Hernan Cortés the Spanish conquistador and explorer who would conquer Aztec Mexico between 1519 and 1521.

FAST FACT Francisco Pizarro's illegitimate birth and poor education left him at a social disadvantage in class-conscious Spain. Throughout his life, his signature was a pair of curling lines between which someone else wrote his name.

Little is known about Francisco's early years. He seems to have had a difficult youth and was poorly cared for. His poor education left him unable to read or write.

I don't care about school. I will be a famous soldier just like my father.

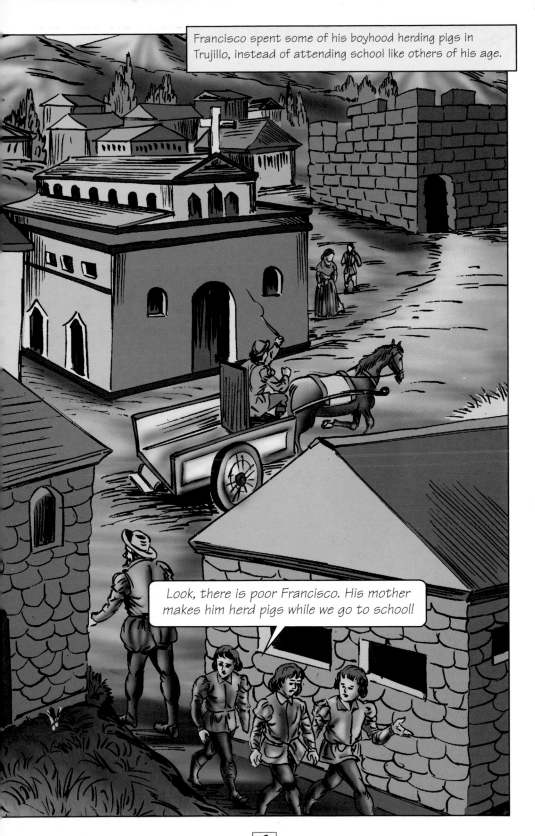

Francisco spent some of his boyhood herding pigs in Trujillo, instead of attending school like others of his age.

Look, there is poor Francisco. His mother makes him herd pigs while we go to school!

Francisco was in Seville in 1492, when the news of Columbus's discovery of the Americas reached Spain. Francisco listened eagerly to the stories told by returning conquistadors.

Admiral Columbus says that the New World is full of gold and silver. Every young man who wants fortune and fame should travel across the Ocean Sea.

Is it possible? How can someone like myself travel to the Americas?

Francisco was inspired by the stories he heard. It was not until the age of 27 (in 1502), however, that he sailed for the Americas to seek fame and fortune as a conquistador.

Francisco arrived in Santo Domingo, the Spanish capital of the island of Hispaniola (modern Haiti and Dominican Republic). He lived there for ten years, and took part in various expeditions of exploration and conquest.

We have reached Santo Domingo. Here every young man can seek his fortune!

FAST FACT Santo Domingo, capital of the Caribbean island of Hispaniola, was the first stop for many young conquistadors from Spain. Here they made contacts, joined expeditions and sought the backing of wealthy patrons.

In 1510, Francisco met the conquistador Alonso de Ojeda, and decided to join his expedition to the Gulf of Uraba between Colombia and Panama.

So, Francisco. Will you join me on the expedition to Uraba?

Yes, Don Alonso. Your plans for conquest are exactly what I am looking for!

In 1513, Francisco joined another expedition, this time led by Vasco Nunez de Balboa to Panama.

Francisco crossed the Isthmus of Panama with Balboa, and on 27 September, 1513, he was one of the first Europeans to see the vast Pacific Ocean. He also took part in Balboa's terrorising of local Amerindians in search of gold.

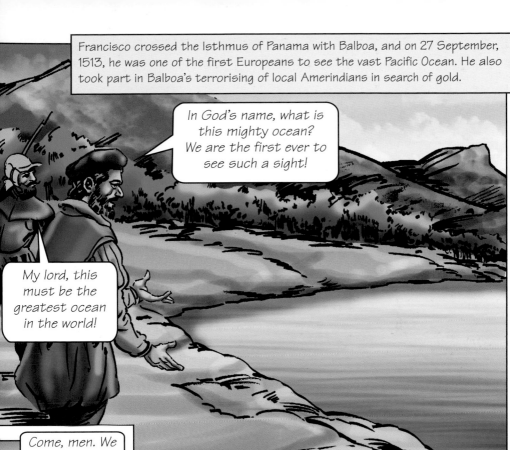

In God's name, what is this mighty ocean? We are the first ever to see such a sight!

My lord, this must be the greatest ocean in the world!

Come, men. We must search out an Indian village and look for gold!

Francisco was given some land in Panama as a reward for his services, and for a while he settled into the life of a cattle farmer.

Francisco's peaceful life was to change, however, when he heard of his cousin Hernan Cortes's conquest of the Aztec Empire in Mexico in 1522. Soon afterwards he heard rumours of wealthy lands south of Panama.

Francisco, Francisco! Great news! Your cousin Hernan Cortés has conquered a great empire in Mexico. He is the richest man in the world!

Come, tell me the story. I am hungry for news of Hernan!

Hernando de Luque

These stories of gold we have all heard have made up my mind! I think we should plan an expedition.

FAST FACT Pizarro was inspired by the tales of the astonishing wealth of gold discovered by his cousin Hernan Cortés in Mexico. Like most conquistadors, however, he needed the support of others to plan and finance his own expeditions.

In 1524, Francisco joined forces with the conquistador Diego de Almagro and a priest named Hernando de Luque in a partnership to explore the western coast of South America. They decided that Pizarro would command the expedition, Almagro would provide the food and soldiers, and Luque would raise money. All agreed to conquer and divide the riches equally.

THE FIRST TWO VOYAGES

Francisco Pizarro's explorations of the north-west coast of South America were a landmark in the discovery and conquest of the continent. The expeditions were joint ventures with other like-minded men, all in search of wealth and power.

On 14 November, 1524, Pizarro and Almagro sailed south from Panama with 80 men. Luque stayed behind to raise more men and supplies.

PANAMA

COLOMBIA

ECUADOR
• GORGON ISLAND
• ROOSTER ISLAND

PERU

■ 1st Voyage
■ 2nd Voyage

The voyage was not a success. The expedition reached only as far as Colombia, and was hit by bad weather and food shortages.

Pizarro's men were attacked by Amerindian warriors wherever they landed. During one battle, Almagro lost an eye when an Amerindian fired an arrow at him.

The expedition suffered greatly and found no gold or silver. Pizarro ordered his fleet to return to Panama. Pizarro's unsuccessful first expedition was marked by the names he gave to places he visited, such as 'Port of Hunger', 'Burned Port' and 'Desired Port'.

In November 1526, after two years preparation, Pizarro sailed again to explore South America. He had 160 conquistadors, and several horses. This voyage reached much further south than the first.

Look at this! They have gold and silver, and boxes of emeralds!

Let us give gifts to these strange men, and see for ourselves their huge ship.

Pizarro's chief pilot, Bartolome Ruiz, captured a large Amerindian balsa-wood raft on the open seas, off the coast of Ecuador.

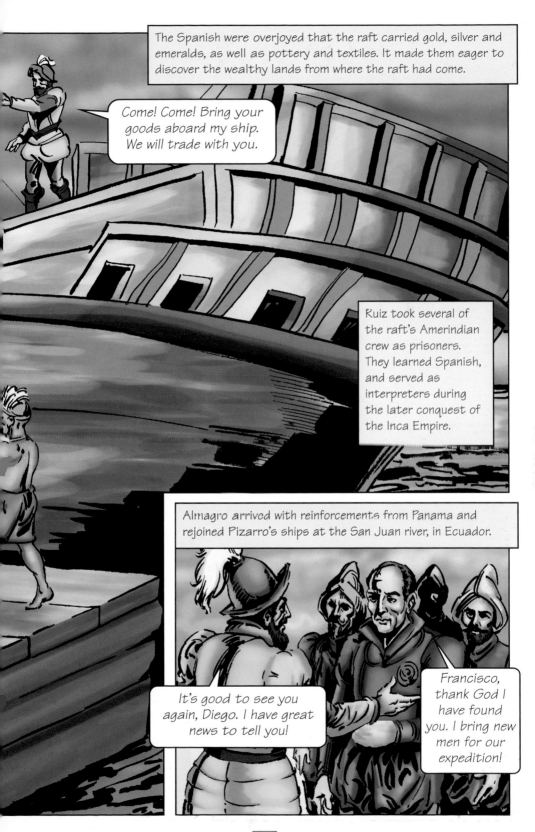

The Spanish were overjoyed that the raft carried gold, silver and emeralds, as well as pottery and textiles. It made them eager to discover the wealthy lands from where the raft had come.

Come! Come! Bring your goods aboard my ship. We will trade with you.

Ruiz took several of the raft's Amerindian crew as prisoners. They learned Spanish, and served as interpreters during the later conquest of the Inca Empire.

Almagro arrived with reinforcements from Panama and rejoined Pizarro's ships at the San Juan river, in Ecuador.

It's good to see you again, Diego. I have great news to tell you!

Francisco, thank God I have found you. I bring new men for our expedition!

Ruiz met up with Pizarro and Almagro and they sailed south. But Pizarro and Almagro argued over the need for even more men. Pizarro decided to remain on Rooster Island with those brave enough to stay with him.

Almagro returned once more to Panama while Pizarro and 13 conquistadors built a small boat and crossed to nearby Gorgon Island, where they waited for 7 months.

Almagro sailed with Ruiz back to Panama. They took with them some of the gold seized by Ruiz from the native raft in order to recruit more conquistadors for the expedition.

Ruiz returned with more men to Gorgon Island and he and Pizarro sailed south to Tumbes in Peru. They were welcomed by the local inhabitants, whose chiefs wore gold and silver jewellery.

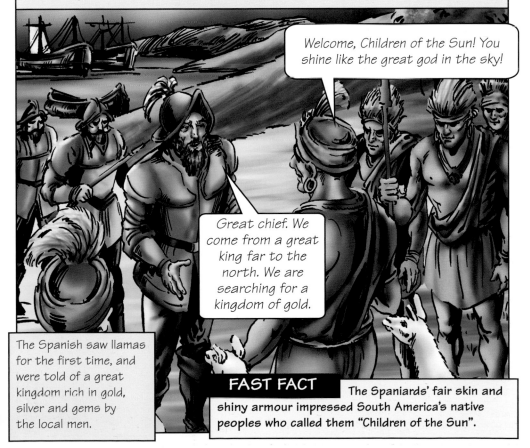

Welcome, Children of the Sun! You shine like the great god in the sky!

Great chief. We come from a great king far to the north. We are searching for a kingdom of gold.

The Spanish saw llamas for the first time, and were told of a great kingdom rich in gold, silver and gems by the local men.

FAST FACT The Spaniards' fair skin and shiny armour impressed South America's native peoples who called them "Children of the Sun".

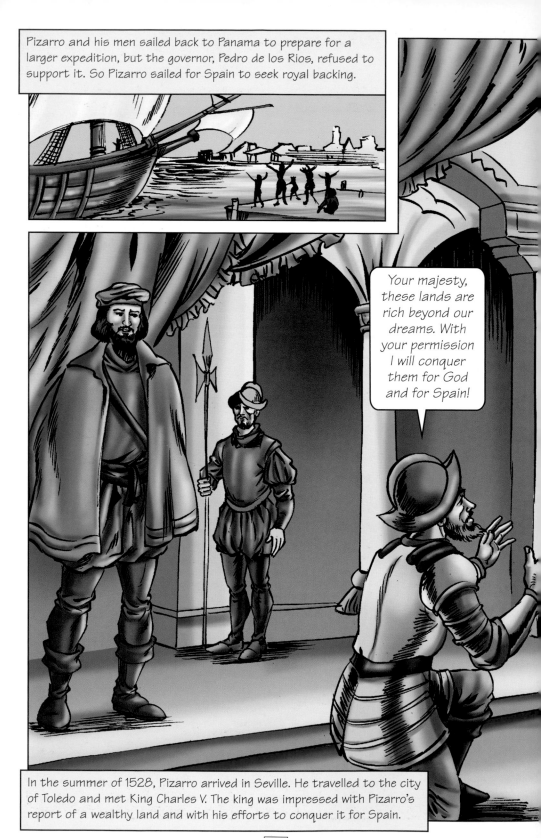

Pizarro and his men sailed back to Panama to prepare for a larger expedition, but the governor, Pedro de los Rios, refused to support it. So Pizarro sailed for Spain to seek royal backing.

Your majesty, these lands are rich beyond our dreams. With your permission I will conquer them for God and for Spain!

In the summer of 1528, Pizarro arrived in Seville. He travelled to the city of Toledo and met King Charles V. The king was impressed with Pizarro's report of a wealthy land and with his efforts to conquer it for Spain.

Charles V gave his permission for Pizarro to lead a third expedition to South America. He instructed Queen Isabella to sign the official documents, and named Pizarro Governor and Captain General of New Castile (now Peru). Pizarro had six months to raise 250 conquistadors. He travelled to Trujillo and convinced his brother Hernando and other friends to join him in the voyage, including Francisco de Orellana who later discovered the River Amazon.

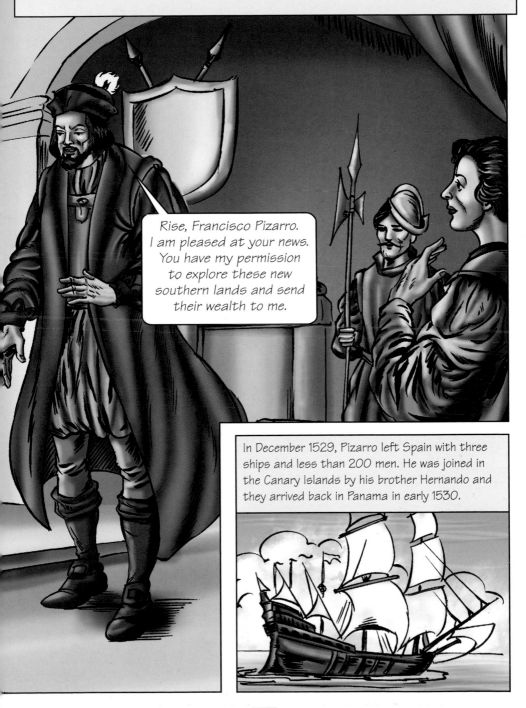

Rise, Francisco Pizarro. I am pleased at your news. You have my permission to explore these new southern lands and send their wealth to me.

In December 1529, Pizarro left Spain with three ships and less than 200 men. He was joined in the Canary Islands by his brother Hernando and they arrived back in Panama in early 1530.

PIZARRO'S THIRD VOYAGE

Pizarro's luck changed on his third voyage, during which he landed in Peru, and discovered and conquered the richest Amerindian civilisation in the Americas. The Inca Empire had about 12 million inhabitants, stretched 4,000 km north to south along the Andes Mountains, and yielded unimaginable quantities of gold and silver.

Pizarro's third expedition left Panama on 27 December, 1530. He sailed first to Ecuador, where he was greeted by Amerindians who gave him gold and emeralds. He sent these back to Panama to help Almagro raise more soldiers.

Pizarro's ships sailed south to Tumbes, but found the town destroyed, and no sign of the conquistadors he had left behind there. Pizarro decided to march inland to avoid trouble and to search for gold.

The Spanish made their way towards the Andes Mountains. On the way they founded the first European settlement in Peru at San Miguel de Piura in July 1532.

FAST FACT On their way to Tumbes, the Spaniards fought a fierce battle with the natives of the Ecuadorian island of Puna. The Battle of Puna killed three conquistadors, and four hundred Amerindian warriors.

From the coast the Spanish could see the majestic Andes Mountains rising up in the east. The next few months would take them on a momentous trek through the Andes to the Inca capital of Cuzco.

An envoy from the Inca emperor, Atahualpa arrived in Pizarro's camp, and invited the Spanish to meet the emperor at the highland city of Cajamarca.

The small Spanish force of only 180 soldiers and 27 horses marched up into the Andes. They travelled for two months before reaching Cajamarca, and found it surrounded by thousands of Inca warriors.

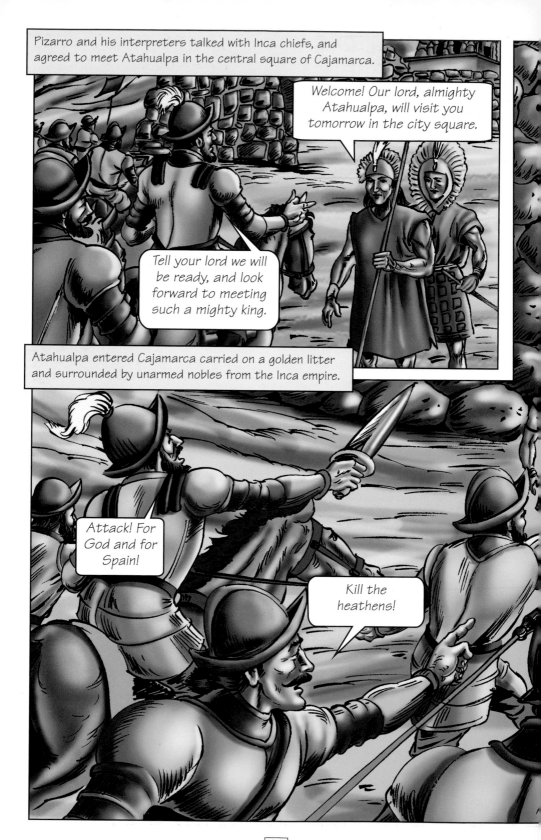

Pizarro and his interpreters talked with Inca chiefs, and agreed to meet Atahualpa in the central square of Cajamarca.

Welcome! Our lord, almighty Atahualpa, will visit you tomorrow in the city square.

Tell your lord we will be ready, and look forward to meeting such a mighty king.

Atahualpa entered Cajamarca carried on a golden litter and surrounded by unarmed nobles from the Inca empire.

Attack! For God and for Spain!

Kill the heathens!

Atahualpa entered Cajamarca carried on a golden litter and surrounded by unarmed nobles from the Inca Empire. But Pizarro had tricked Atahualpa and the meeting was an ambush. Atahualpa did not understand Spanish or the importance of the Christian bible that Pizarro's priest gave him. So when he threw the bible on the ground, Pizarro's forces were outraged! They dragged Atahualpa down from his litter and slaughtered his attendants.

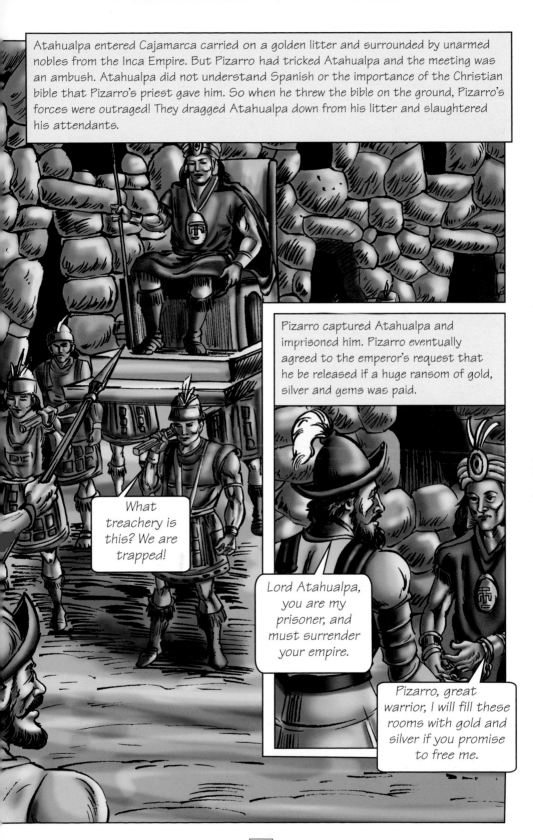

Pizarro captured Atahualpa and imprisoned him. Pizarro eventually agreed to the emperor's request that he be released if a huge ransom of gold, silver and gems was paid.

What treachery is this? We are trapped!

Lord Atahualpa, you are my prisoner, and must surrender your empire.

Pizarro, great warrior, I will fill these rooms with gold and silver if you promise to free me.

For several months Atahualpa's men scoured the empire for gold and silver treasure. They brought it all to Cajamarca, and filled one room with gold, and two with silver. Atahualpa's ransom was paid in full as he had promised Pizarro. But more betrayal was to follow...

Once the ransom had been paid, Pizarro broke his word. Instead of setting Atahualpa free, he had the emperor garrotted on 26 July, 1533.

Pizarro also broke his promise not to destroy the emperor's sacred body so that the Incas could mummify it and worship him. Pizarro ordered the body to be burned.

The Incas wept as Atahualpa's body went up in flames. His remains were given a Christian burial, but later the Incas stole them and hid them in the mountains.

FAST FACT Atahualpa's ransom included priceless gold and silver artworks of the Inca civilisation, which were melted down into ingots. The value of the ingots was immense, but only a fraction of what the original artefacts would be worth today.

CONQUERING THE INCA EMPIRE

Pizarro conquered the vast Inca Empire with only a few hundred Spanish conquistadors – one of the unlikeliest conquests in history. He capitalised on political divisions between two rivals for the Inca throne, ruthlessly murdered the Inca emperor, Atahualpa, took advantage of superior Spanish weaponry and terrorised the Inca people.

Inca Empire

Hernando, brother, you shall have a great share of this treasure for your brave deeds against the Incas.

We are as rich as kings!

Dear Francisco, we shall be the richest men in the world!

Pizarro ordered Atahualpa's treasure of 11 tonnes of gold and 22 tonnes of silver melted down into ingots and shared among his men. A fifth of the wealth was put aside for the Spanish Crown.

Pizarro made a young Inca prince, named Tupac Huallpa, the new ruler. Tupac, however, was really just a puppet emperor under Pizarro's control.

The Spanish then marched south across the Andes towards the Inca capital of Cuzco. The journey lasted three months, and Tupac Huallpa died mysteriously on the way. Pizarro appointed another Inca prince, Manco Inca, as a new puppet emperor.

There may be more Inca warriors ahead, be ready to fight. Keep your guard, men!

Quickly! I do not trust these rope bridges.

Pizarro finally arrived outside the great fortress of Sacsayhuaman which protected Cuzco, and stared in wonder at the huge walls.

FAST FACT The Inca Empire included the Andes Mountains. To rule effectively, the Inca built thousands of kilometres of roads, and huge suspension bridges spanning rivers and ravines.

On Saturday 15 November, 1533, the Spanish entered Cuzco. Large areas of the city had already been burned by the retreating Inca army. Despite this, Pizarro and his men were amazed by the astonishing architecture still standing, with its royal palaces and imposing temples.

We are lost! Our city is destroyed, and the golden sweat of the Sun has been ripped from the sacred temples.

What a city this is! There is more gold and silver here than in all of Christendom.

Pizarro ordered that the city be pillaged, and that every piece of gold and silver be stripped from its buildings and tombs.

Soon after the looting of Cuzco, Pizarro took a teenage Inca princess as a mistress (concubine), and she later gave birth to his child.

In the end, Pizarro decided that Cuzco was too far from the Pacific Ocean and contact with Spain. Pizarro left his brothers, Hernando and Gonzalo at Cuzco, and on 5 January, 1535, he founded the City of the Kings (Lima) by the banks of the River Rimac on the coast.

Between 1536 and 1537, Cuzco was besieged by a huge Inca army. The puppet emperor Manco Inca tricked Hernando Pizarro into allowing him more freedom, and he secretly raised an army of 20,000 Inca warriors. Manco's army took the Spanish by surprise!

Now the great Inca Manco is free, we will destroy the strangers who stole our land!

Conquistadors, charge! We must keep the Inca warriors back!

Cuzco's siege lasted ten months, during which the Incas scored many victories. Lima was also threatened by one of Manco's generals, Quizo Yupanqui. The conquistador Alonso de Alvarado arrived in Lima and helped Pizarro defeat the Inca army that had besieged the city.

The Spanish defeated the Incas at the battle of Sacsayhuaman outside Cuzco in May 1536. Although the Spanish controlled the great fortress, Cuzco was still surrounded by hostile forces.

FAST FACT Inca warriors fought Spanish horses with bolas — two or three heavy stones tied together. When thrown at the horses' legs they tripped them over and brought the animal down.

THE SPANISH ARE RESCUED

Francisco Pizarro's brothers were as ruthless as he was. Their lust for gold and mistreatment of the Incas led to a rebellion and the siege of Cuzco. It also led to a civil war with Pizarro's former comrade, but now jealous rival, Diego de Almagro, who returned to Cuzco at this time from a fruitless expedition into Chile.

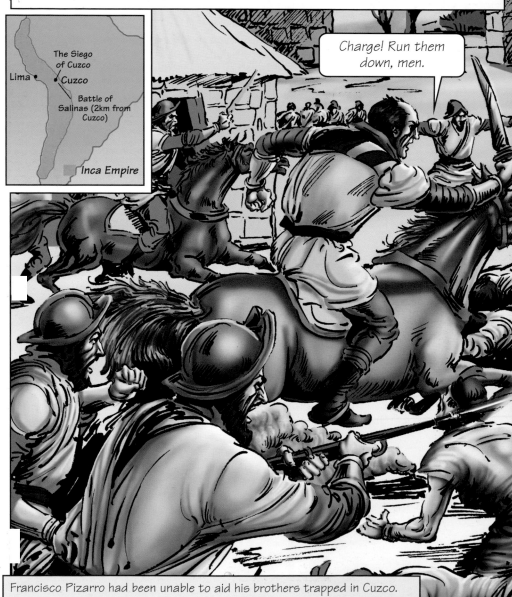

Charge! Run them down, men.

Francisco Pizarro had been unable to aid his brothers trapped in Cuzco. His relief troops had been ambushed by the Incas, and had been forced to return to Lima. On 18 April, 1537, the Inca siege of Cuzco was ended when Diego de Almagro's army entered the city.

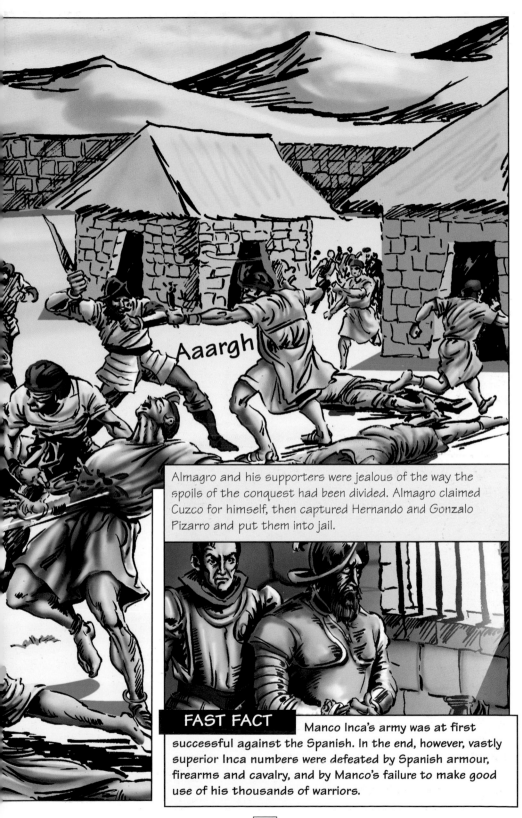

Aaargh

Almagro and his supporters were jealous of the way the spoils of the conquest had been divided. Almagro claimed Cuzco for himself, then captured Hernando and Gonzalo Pizarro and put them into jail.

FAST FACT Manco Inca's army was at first successful against the Spanish. In the end, however, vastly superior Inca numbers were defeated by Spanish armour, firearms and cavalry, and by Manco's failure to make good use of his thousands of warriors.

39

Negotiations began to have Hernando and Gonzalo released. But Pizarro and Almagro's jealousies over the spoils of the Inca Empire could not be resolved. Gonzalo escaped from prison, and when Hernando was released he led an army up from the coast and defeated Almagro at the battle of Las Salinas, outside Cuzco, on 26 April, 1538.

Charge the traitor Almagro! Strike him down for Pizarro and the king!

Almagro was imprisoned in the Inca Sun Temple in Cuzco. His pleas for mercy were ignored and Hernando Pizarro ordered him garrotted and then beheaded.

The tables are turned now, Almagro. You will die tomorrow!

In 1539, Hernando Pizarro returned to Spain, to face charges arising from his execution of Almagro. He was tried, found guilty and imprisoned.

Attack men! We must defeat the Pizarros and claim Peru for Almagro!

Gonzalo Pizarro headed off into the eastern jungles in search of even greater riches. But the expedition suffered great hardships, and Gonzalo returned empty-handed. His comrade Francisco de Orellana continued the expedition, and sailed the length of the Amazon River.

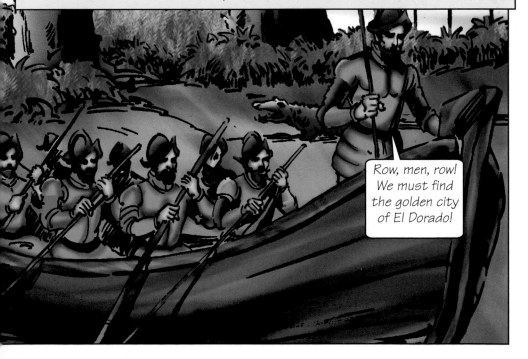

Row, men, row! We must find the golden city of El Dorado!

Diego de Almagro's supporters conspired against Francisco Pizarro in Lima. They hoped to regain power by promoting Almagro's son.

It's agreed then. We shall strike Francisco Pizarro tomorrow after mass!

Yes, and then Almagro's son shall inherit Peru!

On Sunday 26 July, 1541, the conspirators struck. Led by Juan de Herrada, they broke into Pizarro's house and trapped him and several friends in a room. Pizarro fought bravely but could not save himself. Francisco Pizarro was killed by a sword thrust to the throat.

Die you miserable dog!

Justice at last for Almagro and his heir!

Pizarro's body was carried through Lima's main square and taken to the cathedral where it was buried.

Francisco Pizarro, illegitimate and illiterate, conqueror of the Incas and Marquis of the Indies is still buried in Lima Cathedral.

FAST FACT

Apart from his wife and a few close friends, Francisco Pizarro was abandoned by all those he had favoured and enriched. Many wanted to deny him a Christian burial, and hang his body in public instead.

Francisco Pizarro's life began in poverty, but he lived to conquer the largest and richest empire ever created by the native peoples of the Americas. Pizarro's life was full of adventure, cruelty, murder and deception, as well as astonishing feats of bravery and endurance. He was also a victim of his own greed, making an enemy of his collaborator Diego Almagro with whom he fought a civil war, destroying the Inca civilisation, and cruelly mistreating Peru's native peoples.

AD 1475: *Pizarro born in Trujillo, Spain.*

1492: *Americas discovered by Christopher Columbus.*

1502: *Pizarro leaves Spain for the Americas, and spends ten years living on the island of Hispaniola, in the Caribbean.*

1513: *Pizarro joins the expedition of Vasco Nunez de Balboa in the discovery of the Pacific Ocean.*

1514-24: *Pizarro settles in Panama; meets Diego de Almagro and plans voyages to South America.*

1519-21: *Hernan Cortes discovers and conquers Aztec Mexico.*

1524: *Pizarro makes his first voyage south along the coast of Colombia.*

1526: *Pizarro makes a second voyage, and reaches the coast of Ecuador. He stays for 7 months on Gorgon Island.*

1528: *Pizarro sails to Spain to obtain permission for a third voyage from King Charles V.*

1529: *Civil war between Inca emperor Huascar and his half-brother Atahualpa.*

1530: *Pizarro sails south and lands on the north Peruvian coast.*

1532: *Pizarro founds first European settlement of Piura in Peru; marches up into the Andes, and captures Atahualpa at the Inca town of Cajamarca.*

1533: *Atahualpa's gold and silver ransom arrives in Cajamarca; Pizarro executes the emperor, and distributes the ransom amongst the conquistadors. Spanish capture the Inca capital of Cuzco.*

1535: *Diego de Almagro travels south to conquer Chile; Pizarro founds Lima on the Peruvian coast as the capital of New Castile.*

1536-7: *Cuzco besieged by the Inca leader Manco. Diego de Almagro relieves Cuzco, claims it for himself, and imprisons Hernando and Gonzalo Pizarro.*

1538: *Almagro's army defeated at the Battle of Las Salinas by Hernando Pizarro's forces. Almagro is executed.*

1540: *Gonzalo Pizarro leads expedition to the Amazon in search of El Dorado.*

1541: *Francisco Pizarro murdered in Lima by Almagro's supporters.*

DID YOU KNOW?

1 *The discovery of the Americas in 1492 by Christopher Columbus, coincided with the Spanish victory over the last Muslim kingdom in Spain at Granada. Spain had been reunited, and many unemployed conquistadors now looked to the Americas for employment and plunder.*

2 *Most conquistadors were rural Spanish peasants who could neither read nor write. They were tough and brave, but also mainly lusted after gold and women. They were not interested in religious or moral issues, and they treated Amerindians cruelly.*

3 *Most of the gold found in Panama, Colombia and Peru was in the form of sacred statues, masks and jewellery. It was not pure gold but a mixture of gold and copper known as tumbaga.*

4 *The Spanish introduced European diseases to Central and South America. Amerindians had no immunity to such afflictions as influenza and smallpox, and died in their millions.*

5 *The civil war between the Incas Atahualpa and Huascar was caused by their father Huayna Capac dying unexpectedly before naming a successor. He may have died from a European disease that spread to the empire even before Pizarro arrived.*

6 *The Incas regarded their emperors as divine, and called them the 'Sons of the Sun', referring to their supreme solar god, Inti. Gold was called the 'Sweat of the Sun', and silver the 'Tears of the Moon'.*

7 *When Pizarro arrived in Peru in 1532, Atahualpa had recently defeated his rival Huascar for the Inca throne. Atahualpa was on his way to Cuzco to be crowned emperor, and fatefully stopped at the town of Cajamarca where he heard of the Spanish arrival.*

8 *Inca emperors were embalmed as sacred mummies so that they could be worshipped as gods. Atahualpa converted to Christianity so that he would be garrotted as a Christian, rather than burned as an infidel, and thereby keep his body intact.*

9 *Pizarro and his conquistadors were amazed at the efficient organisation of the Inca Empire. The Spanish advanced on Cuzco along Inca roads with way stations (tambos) full of food and clothing, and across huge suspension bridges that spanned canyons and river valleys.*

10 *Pizarro rewarded his conquistadors with shares of Inca gold, silver and gems according to their bravery in battle. To aid the process, he melted down priceless works of art into gold and silver bars or ingots. One fifth was reserved for the Spanish Crown, the rest distributed amongst the army.*

11 *Many Spanish conquistadors took royal Inca women as wives and concubines. The children of these mixed race relationships were known as mestizos, and many became powerful figures in later times.*

GLOSSARY

Amerindians: *The term given to native peoples of the Americas. Columbus called them Indians in the mistaken belief that he had reached India.*

Apu: *Inca lord, or ruler of one of the empire's four administrative regions.*

Arquebus: *An early form of rifle. The powder or shot was loaded into the muzzle of the rifle. Arquebus were used by the conquistadors throughout the Americas.*

Cajamarca: *Inca town in the northern Andes of Peru, built near natural hot springs. Atahualpa had his fateful meeting with the Spanish here.*

Camayoc: *Inca official or craftsman.*

Capac: *Wealthy or influential Inca person.*

Chasqui: *Official Inca messengers, who ran in relays along Inca highways, and passed on news to the next runner.*

Conquistadors: *Spanish soldiers who took part in the discovery and conquest of the Americas.*

Coricancha: *Temple of the Sun God Inti in Cuzco. It was built of the finest quality Inca masonry and its inner walls were sheathed in gold and silver plate.*

Chile: *Name given to the modern South American country that is formed by much of the southern Andes and the adjacent Pacific coast. The area was first seen by Europeans during Diego de Almagro's expedition.*

Coya: *Inca queen or high ranking woman. Coyas were associated in Inca religion with the Moon and silver.*

Curaca: *Inca chief, principal chief of a village.*

Cuzco: *Imperial Inca city located in the Andes of central Peru. Built in the shape of a puma, it had the empire's finest temples and palaces adorned with gold, silver and gems.*

Garrotted: *Spanish form of execution, where a cord is tied around the neck and twisted by turning a stick.*

Gold: *Amerindian gold was usually mixed with copper (and sometimes* silver) to produce the alloy tumbaga, a symbol of sacredness. Europeans, however, were only interested in the pure gold content.

Hidalgo: Spanish term meaning 'Son of a man of social status'.

Inti: Name of the Inca Sun god, the supreme deity and patron of Inca royalty.

Lima: Capital of modern Peru. Originally founded by Francisco Pizarro as the 'City of the Kings' on 5 January, 1535, by the banks of the River Rimac on Peru's Pacific Coast.

New Castile: Spanish name given to the area conquered by Francisco Pizarro, and now occupied mainly by Peru.

Peso: Name given to Spanish coinage. At the time of the conquest, one peso of gold would have been worth about £60.00, and one of silver about £40.00.

Quechua: Name given to the official imperial language used by the Incas.

The Requirement: The reading of an official Spanish document that required any enemy to submit to the Christian faith and the Spanish Crown before an attack was launched – regardless of whether Spanish was understood or not.

Sacsayhuaman: Monumental Inca construction (zig-zag walls and towers) overlooking Cuzco, and made from huge polygonal blocks of stone. Originally a temple, it was used as a fortress by the Spanish and the Incas during the conquest period.

Sapa Inca: Great or Supreme Inca, i.e. the emperor.

Tahuantinsuyu: Literally, 'the land of the four quarters', meaning 'the whole world'. It was the Inca name for their empire.

Tambo: A way station situated along an Inca highway. Its storehouses or 'collcas' were kept stocked with food, clothing and weapons. Tambos were part of the Inca road system that kept the empire together.

Tumbes: North coast Peruvian town, and site of Pizarro's first landing in Peru. Originally pre-Inca, it was taken over by the Incas during their imperial expansion, and later became a colonial Spanish city.

INDEX